THE TALE OF A WANDERING LETTER

TOLD THROUGH 25 POEMS

RAPHAEL JOSE

ISBN 979-888569694-4

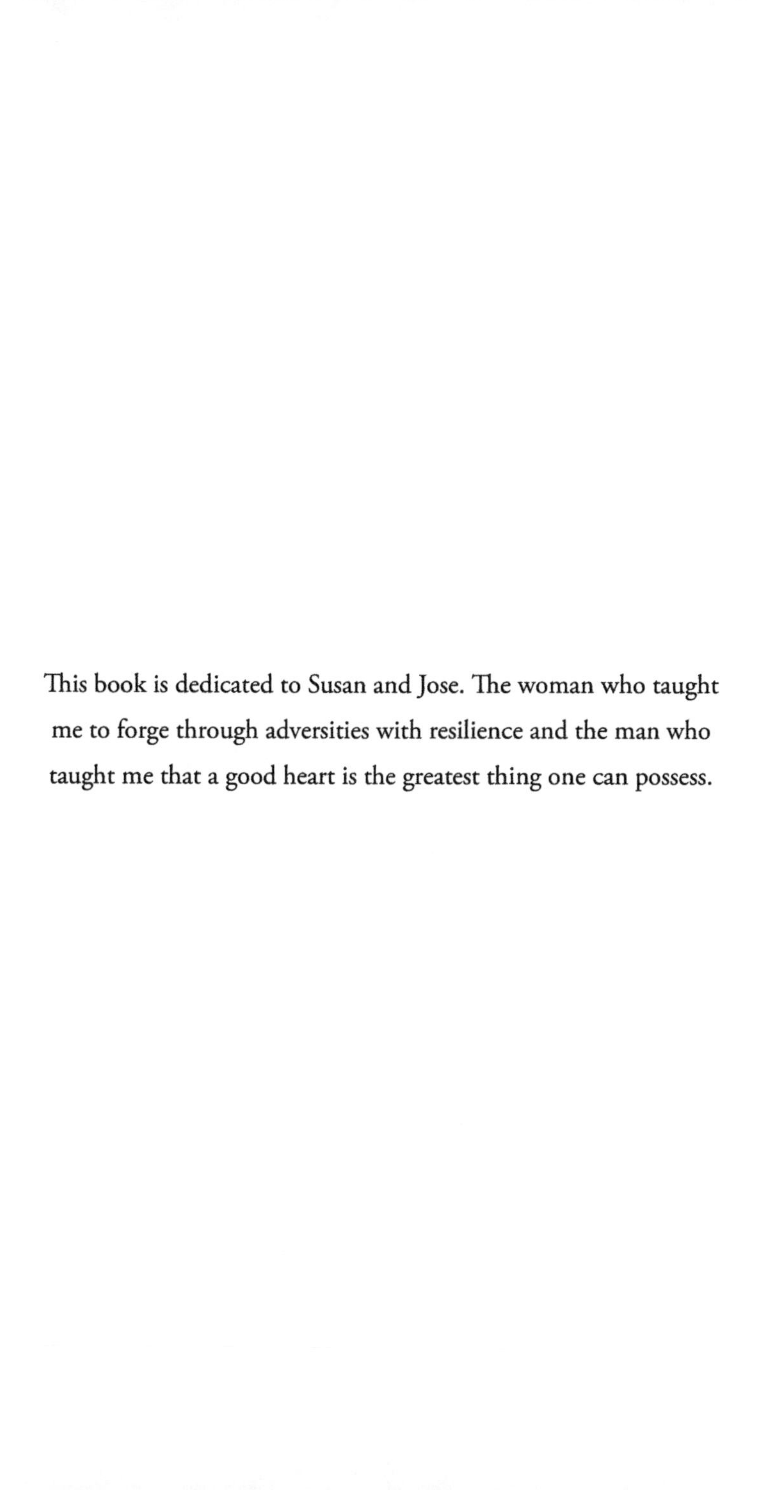

This book is dedicated to Susan and Jose. The woman who taught me to forge through adversities with resilience and the man who taught me that a good heart is the greatest thing one can possess.

Contents

Contents

Preface

The Tale of a Wandering Letter can be seen as a plethora of footnotes, scattered thoughts, memories and unsaid words that were once deemed better forgotten, but have now come together.

These collection of poems written in the past decade were borne through my unexpected meetings with new people and the impressions and residual memories collected from the cities and small towns I have lived in.

This book has inadvertently turned out to be a quest of hope, while I wandered around, with my thoughts bottled up, seeking release in the company of people and places I call my own. Therefore, this letter is an ode to this series of experiences which has elevated this journey of understanding oneself. So, before you bid me goodbye, I entrust you with my newfound hope that you too, shall find a place for yourself.

1. //Why I Left Without Saying Goodbye//

So the first time we met, I was a slightly shy person from the north who took time to shed the layers of insecurities he'd covered himself with. And you being yourself, you were this comforting refuge at a time of despair.

Gradually we formed a bond, a diplomatic one. I decided that I would not tell you that you spoke Hindi rather differently and you decided to teach me how to be warm. I decided that I would not let first impressions deceive me and you decided that you'll teach me how to welcome love back into my heart.

I could never assure you
that I would feel the way you did about life,
warm and passionate,
but eventually you grew on me. Your aura engulfed me and taught me that some days are brighter when one is kind. Some days are lighter when we smile. Every once in a while, I saw you drop subtle hints on how I
could learn to be warmer,
learn to be nicer,
learn to have a heart of gold.
I know we've both faced death and agony,
maybe in different measures, but I believe we are soldiers fighting similar battles at different posts.

I look back to realise you've seen way more than me;
the loss of countless loved ones and the misery of seeing those close,
suffer silently in pain.
Let me tell you the exact moment I fell for you,
the time you held me close while I travelled to work on the first day,
close enough to feel my bones and the muscles that supported them.
Eventually I got used to this peculiar embrace.
To think of the way you introduced me to beautiful people is remarkable-
I finally felt this familiar feeling of being home,
something I had not felt in the longest of times.
And now that I am gone far far away from you,
I want to keep these little moments buried deep within.
I wish to never trade them.
Do you know that there's a part of me that wants to map out every corner of your beautiful expanse, wants to fall over and over in love with your warmth, your beauty, your flaws, your haste, your desire; but I hold on.
It's been a while I have fallen this way but I believe we are meant to fall in love again.
I will come to seek you again in time and rekindle the fire of this love story.
This is not an apology or an excuse.
This is just me telling you why,

Oh, beautiful city of Mumbai,
I left without saying goodbye.

2. //A Letter to the Younger Oggy//

Dear Akku,

You've turned 10 now.

You

have finally learned to ride a bicycle,

while children of your age

are busy doing the so-called bigger things in life.

It is completely okay.

You don't have to feel bad that you had to learn this life skill on a cycle that was not your own.

It's okay, Akku.

In just a decade, you'll realise that

sometimes,

borrowing things from others is going to be tough, things as basic as even time.

Make time for yourself.

You will be happier while you hold on to the little moments that bring joy to your heart.

You have turned 13 now, Akku,

and suddenly you know the weight of losing a parent.

It's like your shoulders have grown stronger in a matter of days.

They've learned to carry the weight of memories from times

gone by.
I know you've seen loss before, yes.
But you will emerge from it.
Like a muscle that grows stronger when it heals from a tear,
you too will eventually regrow these wings that are clipped.
Hold on.
In time, you'll learn that even those who love you dearly
won't be around to fight your battles for you;
you'll learn to fight them alone.
My dear, you are 17 now.
I know you're heartbroken.
You just faced a setback that made you question your passion,
your dreams, your aspirations!
But let me tell you one thing:
You are more than the college you go to,
you are more than the degrees you hold,
you are more than what you have always been told.
In a matter of years, you'll realise that it's not the outside but the inside that defines you. Keep a good heart.
Dear younger Oggy,
you, like everyone is born with a spark.
And if you choose,
you can build a forest fire and light up the world around.
Stay passionate, stay wild, stay untamed.
Run, jump, sing and shout.
Fall in love and fall out of love.
For you are like a fallen star, working your way back to the

galaxy of immense possibilities.

And even though you may collide, you may burn or even explode; don't forget where you have come from.

You're made up of stardust; if you look close enough, you'll see yourself shining.

3. //Heartbreaks//

'Have you ever had a heartbreak?' she asked!
With her eyes piercing every bit of me as I recalled the number of times I had given my heart away, like it was a toy made of clay.
I called it off always, I thought.
'A heartbreak; I don't think so', I said holding onto her hand trying to tell her everything is okay, the pain she felt would go away, sooner than she imagined it would stay!
I left her side thinking about how, over the years, we have grown to believe that heartbreaks happened only when lovers/friends leave or sometimes stay without feelings.
Sitting at a coffee shop, with my mind working slow like an outdated application, I retraced every significant curve I had encountered in my life. So where do I start?
Age 5
Standing at the toy shop, remembering how the wheel of the car Johny had stopped playing with was now broken, I cautiously asked Daddin to buy me a toy.
He said, 'Akku you've got 5 other siblings, you should go and play with them!'
Like a docile puppy, I kept my head down and walked home, with a little tear in my eye that dried before it fell.
Well, what a heartbreak!

Age 7

Sitting at the hospital, getting four nasty injections because a stray dog near my home, found my calf fascinating.

And the doctor trying to be sweet tells me, 'Don't play with dogs, maybe they don't like you!'

I sat there wondering how life would be sad without the friendly woofs and loving licks!

What a heartbreak!

Age 9

Holding the guitar like a bazooka waiting to shoot someone on the first day of music class, only because the drum teacher thought I am too short and my feet won't reach the base pedal and since I was a hyperactive kid, he figured this would trigger me to meddle with the routines of others. Back then, the energy levels in my body could light up some of the deserted streets in Delhi, so beta, you start with the guitar!

What a heartbreak!

Age 12

Watching my father's body being prized in a coffin and lowered to a beautifully decorated grave, I held onto mum's hand, trying to act brave, coz damn, I was 12 and in my eyes I had grown up.

As memories flooded my mind and tears in my eyes, I realised home would not be home without his voice, without his smile. For a while, I froze coz my world made up in a glass had just shattered. Right then, I realized how much his presence had mattered.

My sister said, 'Don't cry, he takes the good ones first. Daddin is in a better place now.'
I knew things would never be the same!
What a heartbreak!
Age 17
Crying in front of my coach like an infant waiting to be fed, the tears I shed were because my really long name never made it to certain colleges' sports list!
What a chance I had missed! Maybe my luck was a little rough, maybe I didn't know the right people to get in touch or maybe I wasn't good enough!
What a heartbreak!
Age 21
While regretting significantly the decisions I had previously made, I tried to make peace with my past. I watched my peers discuss their future plans while I figured how to tackle the 15 exams to call myself a graduate. Indeed, it was a precarious state! Those thoughts of a masters degree, for a while, had been laid to rest!
What a heartbreak!
Right now
I believe I've seen and experienced things which to me, meant greater than a lover leave. All through these, I couldn't find the will to sit back and grieve!
I stand here with a body that has been bruised and broken, a spirit that was destroyed and pushed to the deepest end of the earth's core, a voice that seemed to have lost its way before

it hit the shore, a sight that was shortened by what the world around saw.

Today I stand up, coz I have fallen.

I stand up coz I was lost.

I stand up, never to be crushed again!

Coz I grow, I transform

every second, every minute.

I unlearn to learn.

I withdraw to discover.

I am the creator of my realities,

the preserver of my destiny.

My dear, the next time you ask me: have you ever had a heartbreak?

You know the answer!

'No, I've had experiences and I have always evolved.'

4. //Lionheart//

That day still seems like yesterday.
I cried till I could cry no more, for my head ached and my eyes had turned weary and sore! I remember waiting impatiently to release the earth clutched tight in my palm, as I watched you descend calmly into eternal peace!
My eyes closed slowly like your old typewriter's case, with the earth in my hands finding freedom while sharing your place.
You remember those mornings you carried me to the bus stop? Coz I remember resting on your shoulders, unafraid I'll ever drop!
Do you remember the three minute bath you helped me with each morn?
Do you remember the day I fell while making a cup of tea?
Coz I remember all the sweets and cookies you put in my pocket to pacify me!
Do you remember holding onto my finger when they said all science had failed?
Coz I remember you smiling always even though your body ailed.
You touched lives I can't count on my fingers, and each day in us six, I see your spirit still lingers.
Back then, I thought heroes existed only in comic dreams, within the extravagant settings and elaborate scenes.

Now I've realized I was always with a hero.
Someone who knew what sacrifice really means.
And now those 12 years I spent with you are more than it seems!
'Follow where your heart will lead'-
you told me each day in that hospice, as I left your side with that daily kiss.
As you now charm the cosmos and the being supreme, I find you living everyday in each of my dreams, that have been carved on truth and inspired by wisdom, for you were there all throughout, believing in what I wished to become! I write you this today not because of who I am now, but because of what you will always remain to me.
That day still seems like yesterday.
I cried till I could cry no more!
But now I realize, it was only your body that the coffin managed to prize.
Because your soul is present everywhere I go,
even if it be across the world, to the outer space or to the earth's core.

5. //When Things Get Better//

When things get better,
I will write you a poem.
Not like the ones you've read all along,
scribbled on tissue papers and tattered notes.
Not like the ones that use carefully lettered words
put together with rhymes in articulated spaces,
but a poem filled with feelings;
feelings of joy and comfort;
feelings that remind you,
that like everything else,
this too shall pass.
And though this may seem like a shipwreck,
believe me, it's rough weather and you will sail through,
for you are like a wildflower that grows
from concrete floors.
And I agree this is a rainstorm.
But I know you'll swim through to dry land.
When things get better,
I will send you a letter.
Not like the ones tucked away quietly in your drawer,
with stamps and dates from years ago.
Not like the ones that make you want to cry,

about time that was lost in pain and hopelessness,
but a letter filled with hope.
Hope that brings contentment and peace.
Hope that reminds you
of all the bright and sunny days
that are yet to come.
And though this may seem like the apocalypse,
believe me,
we will learn to rearrange ourselves.
And you are like water that flows,
even through the rocks on mountain tops.
And I agree this is an emergency.
But I know you'll fight time and this space.
Till then, hold on
to the hope clinging on to the words I send you-
as a reminder in times such as these-
however dark or hopeless it may seem,
things will get better.

6. //Remains//

Somedays I swing by those streets,
where we walked together,
to see if stars still danced above me.
Do you know?
The streets in Purani Dilli,
where those winter evenings would collide with the night sky,
still send shivers down my spine.
But I visit them anyways,
just like I visit the memories
we ended up creating for ourselves.
Over time, my dear,
longing can melt into melancholy.
Somedays, I spend evenings waiting
on cold park benches,
to remind myself how it felt to hold you close.
Do you know?
That store I called 'Paris' feels empty now.
It feels like it's found a way
to be at peace with the emptiness and silence,
the same way we've made peace,
and learnt to live with the premature departures,
by eventually moving on.

Somedays, I visit places,
that are lost in time,
only to daydream and smile through my eyes.
Do you know?
The rooftop coffee shop
has now changed.
The outside is shut for everyone,
just like my heart.
But I still visit the coffee shop,
hoping that someday it'll open up.
Even if it doesn't,
maybe someday I'll.
Purani Dilli remains familiar.
Paris remains familiar.
The coffee shop remains familiar.
And yet, you and I, are now strangers.

7. //A Note to a Brave Person//

(Trigger Warning - Anxiety)
It's been a while
that you and I,
are not 'we' anymore,
and don't melt into each other's arms like the ice cubes
we'd put into whiskey glasses,
as we drank away those late winter evenings.
It's been a while
that I have learned to claim comfort holding onto nothing,
but the rhythm of my own breath.
It's been a while
I have thought of writing about everything you'd said in mumbles and whispers.
It's been a while,
I've been meaning to unwind
the sands of time and our lives.
Unwind them just enough to reach that street,
where we met that fateful evening.
I want to unwind just enough to that moment,
when we shared an embrace.
I want to run into your arms like the prodigal son returning home,

and breathe in the alcohol
that ruled your breath.
I want to find my way back to the days
when we'd find comfort in our voices,
where we had built emergency shelters
that would help us travel distances of space and time.
I want to find my way back to that day when anxiety gripped you,
right in the middle of the street.
I want to tell you 'everything is fine,
and all you need to do is hold my hand,
and just breathe.'
Believe me, when I say this,
I know now how it feels
to be stuck between crossroads of self-destruction and insignificance,
pain and desperation.
I know how it feels
to not know which will arrive knocking at my door first:
the anxiety or the night,
breathlessness or sleep.
I know how it feels
to see people enter your life
and walk out like this was an emotion dispensing machine.
I know how it feels
for this body to be buried in a grave of regrets.
And somedays I wish,

I could carry my bed down to the seashore and sail away on a ship that never returns.
Somedays I wish
I was stronger,
strong enough to jump my way out of this.
Somedays I wish,
I didn't have to rip apart bit by bit,
my fingertips,
while I struggle in this cacophony of wildfires that engulf my mind.
It has been a while
that we haven't spoken,
but somedays I wish
I could hold you,
look you straight in the eye and say,
'You are a brave person and
I am proud of you.
Forgive my ignorance,
I now know firsthand,
what anxiety feels like.'

8. //Separation//

I wish I could write
my way through these days,
where time folds itself into memory boxes,
as it signals to me
to let go of uncertainty;
the uncertainty I often hold onto,
like a medallion.
You and I,
sometimes feel like the silence of the day,
and restlessness of the night,
each resolute in their own way.
Divided by realms,
I feel perhaps we were crossroads
that shared momentary spaces of comfort,
which emerged from a yearning to be complete.
And now there's distance between us
that broadens with every passing heartbeat.
So I tell myself 'separation is art',
in an attempt to find ways to melt thoughts into words.
Coz I have always wanted to write to you, about you.
But these words often break into stubborn bouts of silence,
like the night crawling away slowly to make way for dawn.
Dawn, that quietly folds itself with hope in the rays of the

sun,
that speaks of something new.
Yet here we are,
stuck waiting in our yesterdays,
wanting silently for the dawn we once saw,
to finally arrive.

9. //You and I//

As for me, I know I am
an off-season rain shower
that knows its time is yet to come.
A firebird in flames
that knows from the ashes it'll be reborn.
But you, my friend, will remain
a fleeting moment
that sank the earth beneath my feet.
(A goodbye kiss,
that made me want to stay.)

10. //If I were a Poem//

If I were a poem,
I know not where best I would fit.
Coz everyday
is new and always so different.
Somedays, I am an ocean floor
that feels the tremors,
that hit the earth's core.
On other days,
I am a dry rock
that lies deserted at some corner of a sidewalk.
Maybe I'd be a haiku
of three lines with words,
put together in craft,
building myself slowly,
from a storm struck ship
to a safely sailing raft.
If I were a poem,
I'd want to be a gentle one-
one that weaves the night into the day.
And maybe you'd take out time
and stop by
to read between these lines-
lines that paint pictures of rainbows and ecstasy,

in coffee table conversions,
put together with dramatic fantasy.
Coz somedays I feel like the albatross,
hanging on lifelessly.
On other days, I feel like the sailor,
carrying remorse deeper than what these eyes can ever see.
Somedays, I'm power, strength and love
like Angelou (Maya Angelou) and Pope (Alexander Pope).
On other days, I'm misplaced art
that feels more like Hemingway (Ernest Hemingway) and Plath (Sylvia Plath).
This is not a stop sign or a warning call.
Neither is this a well-worded letter or plea.
This is just a yearning filled with hope and imagery-
a wish that the universe might put together for me.
Coz somedays I sit down with myself,
and really wish
I were a poem.

11. //Linguist: What If//

My sister feels I am a linguist.
She believes I have the ability to pick up languages,
like a perfumer picks flowers from a garden,
to create an essence that ends up connecting people to memories.
I speak 4 languages,
yet sometimes,
I find it hard to connect with either of them.
Over the years, I've fought battles with my mother tongue,
for it seems like a roller coaster I wished to never ride on;
and the language I am used to thinking in
is sometimes a jigsaw puzzle I wished I never had to solve.
And for the others,
I can't be without them,
so I hold them close,
hoping they protect me from drowning in a sea of ignorance.
So I save myself in conversations with nothing but a:
- Yes, I get that - (English)
- Haan haan, theek hai - (Hindi)
- Manne te samjh mei agya ji - 'I understand' (Haryanvi)
- Enikyu mansil aayi - 'I understand' (Malayalam)
Yet there are other times,
times when I am speechless,

times when I scream out loud but I barely make a sound.
I speak 4 languages.
Yet I couldn't find words that conveyed love and hope,
when my mother mentioned she had battled depression and anxiety.
I speak 4 languages,
but I never knew how to say I'm sorry,
when a lover realised I had ended up growing out of love.
I speak 4 languages.
Yet on countless occasions, words feel like live canonballs
lying loose in battlefields
that find home in my belly.
And sometimes they rush up my oesophagus
waiting to explode.
But a touch to the farthest end of my little tongue and they freeze,
like snow settling down on mountains in the north.
And so I put up a blank stare,
coz it feels like I've just chewed on a 100 grenades,
and staring away
was the only way of stopping myself from exploding.
So I take a deep breath to remind myself,
that I am learning slowly but steadily.
Har din naya aur alag hoga. (Everyday is new and different)
Aar raat ne ghana andhera bhi ho jya.
Te bakhat ne suraj zaroor kadega. (However dark the night shall be, the sun will rise in the morning)

Nyan ippol padikyu aanu. (I am learning now)
My sister feels I'm a linguist,
yet sometimes when I need most,
in all the languages I speak,
I fail to find words to express.

12. //Lost//

On somedays I rise before the sun,
to travel across roads that are desolate.
Figures in silhouettes dance across me shapelessly,
as I move through spaces in my mind with the help of time.
Somedays I wake with a yearning to feel,
feel the life that runs within my bones.
I look around for signs of hope,
hope that is a reminder of the brighter days to come.
Somedays I visit the beach near the place I live,
to watch the waves waltz with the wind blowing at dawn.
As the salty waves wash away the impression of my feet,
I wish it leads me on to waters of experience.
Lonely roads,
sunrises,
and the 6 AM wind-
all act like companions,
as I attempt to find home in a place I once belonged.

13. //Layers//

I
want to peel off these layers,
layers that have covered my mind
at times when all I want
is the sweet feeling of belonging.
Layers that smother all the hope within me,
in dark alleys made of thoughts,
where I'd never want to be alone.
I want to use just my fingertips to pick them out,
the way you pick words and spread them out
in little notebooks tucked away in quiet corners.
I want to pile these layers,
every one of them,
one on top of the other,
the same way you pile up Lego blocks,
on quiet Sunday mornings,
with laughter and promise.
I want to pour gasoline all over these layers,
the way you pour yourself out,
in midnight conversations with the moon.
I want to set fire to these layers,
letting the flames burn into me,
like candles that never see the light of the day.

I want to peel off these layers,
that bind me-
slowly, steadily, eventually.

14. //To Darwin//

Someday you'll pass through those streets,
where you walked to keep the dream alive,
recalling words and perfecting the beats,
with the dream being your only drive.
Someday you'll pass the red building,
where unknowingly you inspired many,
teaching their souls to youthfully sing,
as they discovered more of themselves they knew!
Someday you'll recall those days of pain,
when your words and deeds were misunderstood,
when your efforts seemed dampened by the rain;
though your heart remained better than good.
Someday you'll step onto the world's stage,
with the crowd cheering in the background,
with your name inscribed in history's pages,
and hearts waiting to be lost in your sound.
Someday you'll rise to make that speech,
about the efforts you put into the dream.
For of your life one can surely preach,
as humility in you always reigns supreme.
Someday in the morning you'll rise,
with the dream finally fulfilled.
You'll glance with pride to the skies,

with gratitude for the belief that was instilled.
Till that day, my friend, don't give up.
For this fight, your dream is true.
Each time you find yourself with a hiccup,
remember, Darwin, we believe in the dream and in you!

15. //Her Strangeness//

Her strangeness is like daylight that brings with itself a certain sense of a new beginning.
It knows how to find you a smile, when your body is shivering like it were stuck bare in the middle of an avalanche.
It knows how to assure you, to breathe when your mind is breaking into unknown pieces of anxious thoughts.
Her strangeness is like a lengthy shadow, that keeps away the heat that pierces your skin.
It lets you finally want to be lost, in the comfort you've always desired with every passing hour.
It lets you forget about the lost time, that can neither be changed or replaced, but only be remembered as an experience.
Her strangeness is like an unknown universe in itself, where stars gradually shed their light compassionately.
It teaches you to slow down sometimes in the middle of all the madness, to realise there's beauty in the chaos.
It teaches you to accept who and what you are, like a precious stone sought by every jewel collector.
Her strangeness has me enthralled and I, like a wanderer, now wait, to find that part of me that's found its way into the unknown.

16. //The Room//

The tiny patch that was invisibly thatched
in this shrinking room,
is now slowly wearing out.
The winter evenings
have managed to bring the cold winds,
travelling outside,
inside.
And spring was brief yet kind,
so kind that this growing patch,
was for a while, forgotten.
And now summer is here,
with long and hot days;
yet everyone, everything seems cold.
In all honesty, I must tell you:
I know not what will remain
of this dilapidating room,
once the monsoons are gone.
It's been a while,
and I thought you should know-
the room you left too soon
is now shrinking.
Winter, spring, summer and monsoon,
turn into years as they pile on,

and now this patch is proving irreparable.

17. //In a Parallel Universe//

I will drown myself in an ocean of hope.
Everyday I'd swim across
to shores of possiblities,
putting myself together each time I meet-
these waters of experiences.
In a parallel universe,
I will write to myself,
knowing that these thoughts don't belong to me,
with a yearning to find words,
that mean something significant.
In a parallel universe,
there will be light around us.
And I'd want to learn
the art of patience and resilience-
letting myself heal to appreciate this journey.
Will you join me in a parallel universe?

18. //I Did Listen//

I was,
while I was lost in the light that emerged from your lips,
as words were spelt out in tender spots.
I was,
as I was breathing in the comfort that rests in your eyes,
which converts this tiny space into a monument of love.
I was,
while I slowly sank into the cosmos of your aura like the last leaf hanging from a wilting tree,
in complete surrender.
Yes, I was listening.

19. //Day Before. Yesterday. Today//

Day before,
I caught myself overthinking.
Most days, it's the weight of aspirations
getting a hold of me.
Though this day was different,
it was the faint sounds
of your shy laughter in my mind
that made its way into my ears.
You see, sometimes we grow out of people,
not because the emotion fades,
but because there's too much of it.
And too much of everything can be injurious:
sugar, salt, joy and longing.
Yesterday,
I sang myself to sleep.
You see, on some nights,
I become Freddie and flow away into motionless dreams.
But this day was different.
Your conversations were the lyrics and your eyes the music.
I realise now that I seem to run out of tune,
coz distance, my dear,
teaches one to see things objectively.

And now I learn that even absence is golden.
The absence of expectations, wait, excuses and pain.
Today,
I didn't talk much,
coz words now feel hollow.
They don't end up painting thoughts.
So I stack them up randomly,
the way you keep your books
in quiet corners, hoping that one day,
someone will read them.
Someday, you will read them,
with patience,
the patience that helps one heal, grow, evolve and shine.

20. //Simple Ways to Stay Away from Someone//

Don't tell her she's beautiful; she's heard that a million times before.

Don't tell her that the moon descends on her face when she smiles; and those eyes, those eyes can replace lighthouses on the seashore.

Don't tell her you miss her; she's heard that a million times before.

Don't tell her that time stops when you're around her and when she speaks, even an exhausted marathon runner will be filled with vigour and joy.

Don't tell her that her words seem like prayers that you wish to let out to God even though you're an agnost.

Don't tell her you can't wait to meet her again; she's heard that a million times before.

Don't tell her that you often think of her laughing and sometimes catch yourself smiling.

Don't tell her you think of what she'd be doing and sometimes catch yourself wandering.

Don't speak to her about how she inspires you, how you pick up cues for your own self from her experiences and learn life lessons through the conversations you share.

Don't talk to her about your aspirations and your deepest

fears, how you feel that time flies like a stringless kite to the realm of the unknown.

Don't ask her if she wishes to speak about the mad day at work. You know you'd be happy to hear those lips speak even while your mind is hazy and exhausted.

Don't tell her she's always welcome to find a hug after a tiring day. You know her warmth is addictive, making you crave for it each time you're away.

Don't assure her you're around if she wants to speak to someone. Even though you know that's a way of knowing the countless things that cross her mind in that moment.

Don't help her with your concern and care. Even though you know that's the way you're wired and you can't help but care for her well-being.

Don't hope for her to find what she desires. Coz she's a soldier who's literally fought demons - outside and inside; she will get there with or without you.

Don't cook for her, the meals she's been craving to eat. Coz she's a traveller and can make do with whatever she gets.

And don't you ever dare write a poem for her, coz many have written for her in the past and yet managed to break her heart.

Keep everything you want her to know locked away in a memory box and drop it into the sea the next time you're at Marine Drive.

But if, and I reiterate, if you ever happen to do, say or mean any of these, don't forget to tell her you might be falling for her and can't stay away from the thought of her each moment.

21. //Dear Mother//

Dear Mother,
I am done fighting
with you and the rituals you've grown up on.
I'm done fighting
against the idea of fellowship.
Mother, in the past few years,
I have realized that
some battles can be fought
without resistance.
I have realized that
some fights can be undertaken
in solitude.

22. //Hey There//

Hey there
I don't want to think
of all the things that have passed
and the magic that you once had
in your tightly-held fists.
But here I am,
wandering in the streets of wonder
that lead to the district of melancholy,
hoping our paths cross, again.
I wonder if you still raise your eyes
in prayers scattered like dew,
all over the universe?
Are you still staring at the moon
in silent yet meaningful monologues,
written as the day turns to night?
Do you still rub your palms,
creating and destroying atoms at random -
the same way you treat words?

23. //Wildflowers//

Come, let's be like wildflowers that grow
in terrains that are foreign and conditions that are hostile.
Let's watch ourselves heal those bruises, while catching a glimpse of the rising sun, that makes way for a new day.
Come, let's be like wildflowers - those that are signs of hope in times of despair and feelings of turmoil.
Let's awake from our slumbers, of a cautioned life and calculated risks, to embrace everything that this magical journey entails.
You are a traveller. You know wildflowers are beautiful.
Come, let's be them.

24. //Wishlist//

If I could write myself a wishlist,
hope would find its place
right at the top.
It's been a while
since the days have gotten longer.
Yet the insignificance of these nights
is slowly growing stronger.
It's night now and I
wish to stargaze.
Though the sky is a subtle reflection of the heart,
covered with clouds of doubt and a moon of
aspirations,
I want to write it all,
on letters and tiny frames.
But today has been long.
I guess I'll just sit back,
break from fighting demons,
within and without,
only to just breathe.
Coz if I could write myself a wishlist,
hope would find its place,
right at the top.

25. //Homecoming//

The last time, you and I, we met,
I saw your eyes read stories of departure
that were like novels written with pain
buried deep within my heart.
I held you close, looking into your soul,
and kissed you goodbye,
knowing deep within, that this,
was not an end to our story of love.
Days have passed, while seasons have changed,
and maybe I have as well.
Yet you, my lost love, have not changed a bit,
and these feelings too are the same.
So here I come, to fall in love again,
and rekindle the fire that got blown away.
No apologies, no excuses, no settling for less.
Take me as I am.
I'm coming back, dear love. I'm here to stay.

Author's Bio

Raphael Jose is an actor and poet, who believes hope can be found even in dark places. His pieces often engage with emotions and are mostly personal yet connected to everything around him. He likes to travel and is particularly fond of experimenting with food.

9 798885 696944

Printed by Libri Plureos GmbH in Hamburg, Germany